# KEEPING PETS

# Cats

Louise and Richard Spilsbury

www.heinemann.co.uk/library
Visit our website to find out more information about Heinemann Library books.

To order:
☎ Phone 44 (0) 1865 888066
▤ Send a fax to 44 (0) 1865 314091
▭ Visit the Heinemann bookshop at www.heinemann.co.uk/library to browse our catalogue and order online.

First published in Great Britain by Heinemann Library, Halley Court, Jordan Hill, Oxford OX2 8EJ, part of Harcourt Education.

Heinemann is a registered trademark of Harcourt Education Ltd.

© 2006 Harcourt Education Ltd.

Editorial: Andrew Farrow & Dan Nunn
Design: Richard Parker and Q2A Solutions
Picture Research: Erica Newbery
Production: Chloe Bloom

Originated by Modern Age Repro
Printed and Bound in China
by South China Printing Company

10 digit ISBN: 0 431 12424 8
13 digit ISBN: 978 0 431 12424 7

10 09 08 07 06
10 9 8 7 6 5 4 3 2 1

**British Library Cataloguing in Publication Data**
Spilsbury, Louise
  Cats. – (Keeping pets)
  1. Cats – Juvenile literature
  I. Title II. Spilsbury, Richard
  636.8
A full catalogue record for this book is available from the British Library.

**Acknowledgements**
The publishers would like to thank the following for permission to reproduce photographs:

Alamy pp. **4t** (Rodger Tamblyn), **10t** (Marc Hill); Ardea pp. **5**, **7t** (Francoise Gohier), **20b**, **23t**, **33** (Dominic Burke), **39t**; Ardea/John Daniels pp. **7b**, **8t**, **8b**, **9b**, **10b**, **11**, **13**, **18t**, **19b**, **20t**, **21b**, **25**, **29**, **31**, **34t**, **35**, **36**, **38**, **39b**, **42**; Corbis p. **41** (James L. Amos); Dan Nunn p. **45**; FLPA pp. **15t** (Foto Natura Catalogue), **17** (Mark Hamblin); Getty Images p. **32** (Photonica/Diane Collins); Harcourt Education Ltd/Tudor Photography pp. **14**, **18b**, **23b**, **24**, **26**, **27**, **28t**, **28b**, **29t**, **43**, **44**; NHPA pp. **6** (James Warwick), **9t** (Yves Lanceau); Photolibrary pp. **4b** (Index Stock Imagery/Fotopic), **12** (Survival Anglia/ Marianne Wilding), **21t** (Botanica/Satushek Steve), **30** (Keith Ringland), **34b** (Index Stock Imagery/Pat Canova); Punchstock pp. **1** (Corbis), **19t** (Corbis); Richard Parker p. **22**; Ron Kimball p. **15b**; RSPCA pp. **16** (RTL), **37**; SPL p. **40**.

All additional incidental images used courtesy of Getty Images/Photodisc.

Cover photograph reproduced with permission of Ardea/John Daniels.

The paper used to print this book comes from sustainable resources.

# Contents

Any words appearing in the text in bold, **like this**, are explained in the Glossary.

# What is a cat?

Do you know anyone with a pet cat? The chances are that you do, because cats are one of the most popular pets in the world.

## A type of mammal

Like us, cats are a type of mammal. Mammals are **warm-blooded** animals that have hair on their bodies. Female mammals can feed their young with milk from their bodies. Unlike people, all cats are **carnivores.** This means that they have strong, sharp teeth, which they use to kill other animals.

When a cat yawns, it shows off its sharp teeth. All carnivores have teeth like these for eating meat.

Cats can be very friendly pets that make you feel special. But you need to look after them!

## Need to know

- It is up to you and your family to take care of your pet. You must give your cat enough food and water. You must help to keep him clean, healthy, and safe.
- It is cruel not to care for pets properly. There are laws in many countries to protect cats and other animals from cruelty.

4

## How did cats become pets?

All pet cats are descendants of African wild cats. In the past, people probably first kept wild cats to protect their food supplies. Cats are very good at hunting mice and other **rodents** that eat stored grain. Over time, some wild cats became domesticated. This means that they became more tame and more comfortable living in people's homes.

In the 18th and 19th centuries, people started to collect unusual-looking cats. Explorers from Europe collected cats from other parts of the world, such as Asia. Soon there were many **breeds** of pet cat, which all looked different.

We know Ancient Egyptians kept pet cats because of pictures, sculptures, and even mummies of cats found in tombs!

### Ancient pet cats

Around 4,000 years ago, Ancient Egyptians kept pet cats because they thought they were very special. They worshipped cats as gods and punished anyone who harmed a cat. But these are not the oldest pet cats. **Archaeologists** have found bones in ancient graves in Cyprus that are from pet cats kept 9,500 years ago!

5

# Cat facts

Have you ever noticed that pet cats look a bit like tigers or leopards? This is because they are all members of the cat family.

## Feline features

There are around 36 **species** in the cat family. Most have a long, strong body with a long tail. Their feet are wide with soft pads underneath. They can fold their sharp, hook-shaped claws in and out of the tips of their toes. Cats' heads are usually rounded with triangular or rounded ears, big eyes, and whiskers. Many wild cat species have striped or spotted hair patterns that help them remain hidden as they hunt.

Most cats live in a particular area called a **territory.** Cats scratch and leave special scent marks on trees, posts, and other things in their territory. These signs tell other cats to keep away.

### Did you know?

- Cats usually live for around fourteen years, but sometimes they live as long as twenty years!
- Male cats are called **toms.**
- Female cats are called **queens.**
- Baby cats are called kittens.

Pet cats are related to big cats like this leopard. Both big cats and pet cats spend a lot of time sleeping.

## Kittens

Queens can start having kittens when they are about six months old. A group of kittens born at the same time from one queen is called a **litter.** Each litter may have five or six kittens. When kittens are born, their eyes are closed. Their eyes open after two days. Then the kittens are ready to explore the world around them.

Kittens **suckle** for around five weeks before they start to eat solid food.

### Fun fact
All kittens are born with blue eyes, which then change colour over time!

Cats are very agile. They can leap and twist in mid-air to make sure they catch their prey.

## Clever hunters

Most members of the cat family are excellent hunters. Wild cats need to be good at hunting to make sure they have enough to eat. However, even well-fed pet cats will hunt birds and **rodents** if they get the chance.

Cats have several special features that help them hunt. They find their **prey** using good eyesight and hearing. Cats can see much better than humans even when it is almost dark. They move silently towards their prey on padded feet. Then they run fast to catch their prey with their claws.

# Types of cat

Pet cats can look very different. Some cats come in single colours such as black, white, ginger, blue-grey, or chocolate brown. Others are white with patches of another colour. The other main hair pattern is tabby. Tabby cats usually have thin black lines and dots on a brown background.

Tabby cats have a striped coat.

## Hair type

Most non-**pedigree** (mixed **breed**) cats can have either long or short hair. Some pedigree breeds, such as Siamese cats, always have short hair. Others, such as Turkish Van cats, always have long, silky hair. The Rex cat has short, curly hair. The Sphynx has almost no hair at all but its skin often has patches of different colour!

## Why are striped cats called tabbies?

There was once a type of striped silk cloth made in a place called Al-Attabiya in Iraq. People named striped cats "tabbies" because their hair pattern looked like this cloth!

Tortoiseshell cats have hair in patches of ginger, black, and white. This one is long-haired.

## Shape and size differences

Cats can look different in other ways:

- Siamese cats have very long, narrow heads with long, pointed ears and sloping eyes.
- Persian cats have a very flat face with a short nose.
- Maine Coons are very large and shaggy.
- Manx cats have no tail.

## Pedigree and non-pedigree cats

There are about 80 different breeds of pedigree (purebred) cat. Cats in a breed always have similar-coloured hair and eyes. They always have the same body shape. Carers of pedigree cats usually have written records of the other relatives of their cats.

Non-pedigree cats are a mixture of many different breeds. There are hundreds of different breeds and it is uncommon to have any information about their ancestors.

Russian blues are a single-colour pedigree breed of cat. They always have thick, short, blue-grey hair and green-blue eyes.

Pedigree Birman cats have long fluffy white hair with patches of grey or brown. They always have blue eyes.

9

# Are cats for you?

Cat lovers say cats make the best pets because they are clever, interesting, and very friendly. But not everybody likes cats as pets. If you are thinking of choosing a cat as a pet, you and your family will need to consider both the good and not-so-good points of having a cat.

Cats can be very friendly and loving.

Cats can welcome you whenever you come home.

## Cat good points

- Cats are intelligent and have great personalities.
- Cats can be very playful and can help you to feel relaxed.
- Cats can be good companions.
- Cats are happy to live in smaller spaces than most dogs.
- Cats are usually very clean.
- Cats live a long time.

## Cat not-so-good points

- Cats are very independent and have strong personalities. Some cats are moody and do not like to be handled. Others insist on being near you all the time!
- Cats may scratch and ruin furniture, carpets, and other things in your home.
- Cats are a much longer commitment than pets that live for a shorter time, such as mice or rabbits.
- Cats are expensive to feed and take to the vet.
- Cats may try to kill any pet **rodents** or birds that you keep.

Cats can easily damage things in your home.

### Yes or no?

Are you ready to say yes to living with a pet cat? Do you want to share many years of your life with a clean, intelligent animal? If so, then it is time to think about which cat to choose.

# Choosing your cat

When choosing your pet cat there are several things you will need to consider.

## One or more?

Most cats will happily live alone with a family. However, if your family is away from home a lot, it might be good to get two cats so they can keep each other company. If a cat on its own gets bored, it may start messing up your home!

Of course, two or more cats cost more to feed and care for. They need more space in your home. Like people, cats enjoy their own space from time to time. If you already have an adult cat, watch it carefully if you get a new kitten. Introduce the kitten to the adult gradually or else they may fight. Make sure you give both animals lots of attention.

Adult cats should soon get used to a new kitten in their home.

## Male or female?

**Toms** and **queens** both make friendly pets. Whichever sex of cat you choose, you should have them **neutered.** Neutering is a simple, painless operation carried out by a vet. It stops cats from having kittens. Each year millions of kittens are born that cannot be cared for properly. Many end up in **animal shelters.**

Un-neutered cats often try to wander away from your home and they might get into fights. Un-neutered toms may spray smelly **urine** around your home to remind other cats it is their **territory.**

## What age?

The age of the cat you choose is important. Kittens are usually more playful than older cats, but they need a lot of attention. You will have to teach kittens to use a **litter tray** and not to scratch things.

Adult cats should be **house-trained** and calmer. They may already be used to busy homes. However, some adult cats may not adjust to a new home. Some try to return to their previous home.

### Age limit

Remember that kittens should not leave their mothers until they are at least eight weeks old.

Kittens love playing together, especially if they are from the same **litter**.

## Pedigree or non-pedigree?

Most people have non-**pedigree** (mixed-breed) cats. In general, they are less fussy and less likely to get sick than pedigree (purebred) cats. Non-pedigree cats are easier to find because they are always available at **animal shelters**. They also make great family pets.

Some people choose pedigree cats. Different **breeds** have some typical ways of behaving that may affect whether you choose them as pets. The table on the right shows a few examples. You can find out more about different breeds by checking out the Further Reading section on page 47. Whichever breed you choose, bear in mind that, just like people, all cats are different. Not all cats behave in the typical way for their breed.

## Long-haired cats

You will need to brush long-haired cats every day to keep their hair smooth and tangle-free. Even if you brush them, long-haired cats will still leave hair around your home. It will collect on the floor, curtains, sofas, and clothing. It takes time to clear it up. People with **asthma** or breathing problems should avoid long-haired breeds, because the hairs could affect their health.

**Top tip**
A long-haired kitten usually grows up to become a long-haired adult.

Long-haired cats cannot help leaving hair around your home.

# Know your breed

| Breed | Characteristics |
| --- | --- |
| Birman | Very calm |
| Siamese | Can cause a lot of damage in the home |
| | Has a very loud wailing meow |
| | Demands a lot of attention |
| Persian | Not very active; likes to lounge around |
| Turkish Van | Enjoys water |
| | A large, long-haired breed that does not need much **grooming** |
| Maine Coon | Good with children and dogs, intelligent, and calm |
| | Likes to scratch things, so needs a scratching post |
| Korat | Dislikes sudden, loud noises |

Most Siamese cats are quite demanding. They will try to get your attention when you are doing other things.

Maine Coon cats can get too big for a small or frail person to lift easily. They also eat quite a lot of food.

# Where to get your cat

There are many places to get a pet cat. You could ask friends, neighbours or your local vet to find out if anyone has a cat who needs a home. Vets will only suggest cats that are healthy and from a good home.

Some people choose cats from **animal shelters** or **rescue centres.** Workers in animal shelters check the health of each cat. They may also want to know a lot about your family and home before allowing you to have one of their cats. This is because their job is to make sure that their cats will have happier lives than before. You should choose a rescue cat carefully though. Some rescue cats are nervous because people have treated them badly in the past. It may take time for a rescue cat to trust you.

Cat **breeders** are the people to go to if you want a very particular kind of cat. **Pedigree** breeders keep careful records about their cats. Pedigree cats are expensive, so make sure you go to a respected breeder.

Make sure that the pet shop or cat breeder keeps its cats in clean cages.

Many people buy cats from pet shops, but pet shops do not always know much about the background of the cats for sale. You should ask questions about the cat's age, health, and parents. If the people in the shop do not know much about the cat, you should get your cat somewhere else.

**Top tip**
Be careful when choosing a kitten from a pet shop. If kittens are taken from their mothers too early or have travelled a long way to the shop, they may get sick.

## What to look for

The following tips should also help when choosing your cat:

- Always look for a healthy cat. Check that it has bright eyes, smooth hair, and a clean bottom.
- Try to see a kitten with the rest of its **litter** and its mother. Then you can see for yourself how she cares for them.
- Kittens should be playful and alert. Lively kittens will watch or even come to check out your finger if you wiggle it nearby. More nervous kittens may be scared by it.

Try to see several litters of kittens before you make your final choice.

17

# What do I need?

Before bringing your cat or kitten home you need to have everything ready for him or her. You will need bowls for food and water, and many other things. Most of these things can be bought in pet shops.

**You will need a strong, secure cat basket to carry your cat home or to the vet's.**

## Litter trays

Cats need somewhere to go to the toilet inside your home. Most people use **litter trays,** which are high-sided plastic trays. You should half-fill them with **cat litter.** Cat litter soaks up cat **urine**. Your cat will usually scrape litter over its **faeces** (poo) to cover it up. Most types of cat litter are made of small pieces of clay, paper, corn, or wood. Cat litter also helps to keep the tray smelling fresh.

**A high-sided litter tray stops the cat kicking too much cat litter onto the floor.**

## Cat napping

Most cats sleep for about sixteen hours each day! You should make sure they have somewhere comfortable, safe, and warm to go that is out of draughts. You can buy a soft fleece bed with a roof, but a basket or cardboard box lined with an old blanket is just as good. Choose bedding that can be washed easily and remember that whatever you provide, your cat may still choose to sleep on your bed or sofa!

Cats normally sleep for hours each day in their warm, safe bed.

## Collar

If your cat goes outside, even for a short time, she should have a collar. Reflective collars help motorists see cats at night. Collars with bells warn wild animals that a cat is nearby. The collar should have an identity tag, which will help someone else return your cat if she gets lost. The collar should also have a stretchy (elastic) piece in it, or be a specially made "break-away" collar. This means that if the collar gets caught on something it will slip off rather than hurt the cat's neck.

## Microchipping

Vets can inject a tiny **microchip** under a cat's skin. The microchip holds information that identifies your cat. The best thing about a microchip is that it cannot be removed or accidentally come off a cat if it loses its identity tag or collar.

Identity tags carry information such as your telephone number and the cat's name.

## Scratching posts

Cats need to scratch their claws against rough things to keep them in good condition. Some cats may scratch things in your home. To stop them doing this, provide a scratching post. You can buy many different types or make one out of a tree log that still has its bark on. Cats often like to scratch after waking up, so put the scratching post near their bed.

## Top tips

Does your cat still scratch furniture even after you gave him a scratching post? Here are two things you can try to stop the scratching:

- Spray a little water at the cat as he is scratching.
- Attach orange peel to the scratched area.

Cats do not like water or the smell of orange. Your cat will soon learn to avoid the area!

## Toys

Cats love all sorts of toys. You can buy toys or make them from things you can find around your home, such as balls of string, ping-pong balls, or feathers. Make sure the toys are safe. Do not give cats anything they might swallow, such as elastic bands, or things that catch on their claws, such as fine threads. If you do not know which toy to choose, ask other cat owners what their cats prefer.

Some cats like to play-fight and bat their toys.

Cats love to explore outside. They meet other cats, chase things, climb, and enjoy sights, sounds, and smells.

## Cat flaps

Cats need exercise. If they don't get enough they may become fat and unhealthy. Most cats get exercise by going outside on their own. However, never let a new cat out as soon as you get him home because he might get frightened and run away. This is very important if you live near a road. Keep your cat inside for several weeks. Then go out with him for short periods of time at first, until he is used to the garden.

Many cat owners fit a cat flap to their door. Some cat flaps are locked by a magnet. Your cat wears the magnet key on his collar. The flap only opens when your cat comes near. This stops other cats getting in.

### Top tip

Not all cats know how to use a cat flap. You may need to encourage them through the flap by placing their food bowl on the other side or by taping the flap open!

Cats can come and go as they please through cat flaps without you having to open and shut the door.

# When your cat arrives

Kittens may be more frightened in a new home than adult cats at first, but they usually settle in more quickly.

When you first bring your pet cat home you will need to gently introduce her to her new world.

## A safe house

You need to get a room in your home ready for your new cat:

- Remove any houseplants. Cats can get sick if they chew the leaves of some plants.
- Remove objects that could fall over if the cat jumps on them, such as pots on shelves.
- Keep other pets out of the room for a couple of days. The smell of your other pets will fade, and your new cat will not be frightened by the smell.
- Put down food, water, and a **litter tray.**

## First steps

Next, bring the cat into the room in her carrier. Close all the windows and doors. Open the cat carrier but stay nearby. The cat will eventually explore the room. Never frighten the cat by forcing her to come out. When your cat has explored the room, sit by her. Gently talk to and stroke her to calm her. Then introduce her slowly to any other rooms in your home and any other pets.

## Litter training

Adult cats will often know how to use a litter tray, but kittens need training. Kittens usually need to use the litter tray after eating or sleeping. When your kitten wakes up or finishes eating, gently place her in a tray of fresh **cat litter**. At first she may not realize what the litter is for. Use the litter scoop to show her how to dig it. Praise the kitten each time she uses the tray.

There may be a few accidents before kittens learn to use a litter tray.

## Dealing with a messy cat

If your cat goes to the toilet away from the litter tray, put on a pair of gloves and clean it up. Then try one of these things to stop the cat from doing it again:

- Move the cat's bed to the soiled area. Cats do not like to make a mess in the place where they sleep.
- Spread aluminium foil on the soiled area. Cats do not like walking or sitting on foil.
- Put a **deterrent** spray on the soiled area. You can get this from a pet shop or vet.

It's okay to say "no" firmly but softly to your cat when she does something wrong. But it is also important to praise her when she does something right.

# Taking care of your cat

There are some things you must do to care for your pet cat. You must give it food and water each day and you must clean up after it.

## Prepared food

Pet cats usually eat cat food bought from pet shops, vets, or supermarkets. Cat foods contain meat, some vegetables, and the right balance of **vitamins, calcium**, and other **nutrients** to keep your cat healthy. Food made for other pets, such as dogs, is not good for cats.

You can buy both wet and dry cat foods. Wet food comes in tins or plastic sachets. Dry food looks like small pieces of biscuit. Different types of wet and dry cat food are suitable for cats of different ages. For example, there is special food for kittens and another for old cats. Cats are often fussy eaters, so it may take a little while before you find out what type of food your cat likes best.

## Top tip

Cats like to eat food at room temperature. If you store tinned food in the fridge to keep it fresh, let the food warm up a little before serving it to your cat.

You should feed your cat in a quiet corner of the kitchen where it will not be disturbed while it eats.

## Feeding routine

You should try to feed adult cats at the same time each morning and evening. Kittens need more regular feeding, depending on their age. The following tips should help:

- Put a small amount of food, usually about a third of a cup, in a metal or ceramic (pottery) bowl. These are easier to wash than plastic bowls.
- Place the bowl in the same spot each time.
- Remove any uneaten food from the bowl after mealtimes.

## Water

Cats need to drink fresh, clean water every day to remain healthy. They usually drink a lot after feeding but make sure your cat's bowl is always full. Any bowl you choose should be heavy so it is not easy to knock over. Some people buy special water fountains for cats to drink from.

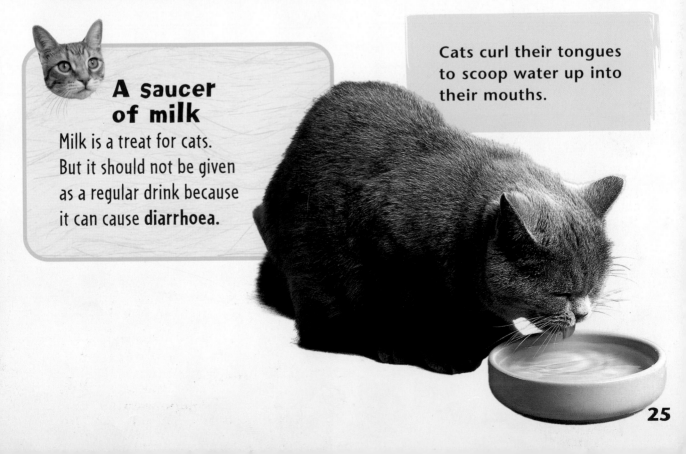

### A saucer of milk

Milk is a treat for cats. But it should not be given as a regular drink because it can cause **diarrhoea**.

Cats curl their tongues to scoop water up into their mouths.

## Fresh food

Some people feed their cats freshly cooked meat or fish. Fresh food gives cats some extra **minerals** and ensures they have a balanced diet. Many people feed their cats a little fresh food once or twice a week to make mealtimes more interesting.

## Cat treats

Many cats enjoy food treats once in a while. Cat treats from pet shops include biscuits and **catnip** drops. Unfortunately, some of these treats contain salt, fat, and chemicals. These things can harm cats if they eat lots of them. Check to find out what is in the treats you want to buy. Then you will know exactly what you are giving your pet.

## Plants for cats

Many cats like to nibble on grass because it contains minerals. Grass also tickles their throat and makes them **vomit**. Many people think cats do this to clear out their stomach from time to time. Cats also like the smell and taste of catnip or catmint. They like to rub against or roll in this plant.

Cats enjoy freshly cooked meat or fish, but remember to remove any small bones before you give it to your cat. Otherwise, the cat could choke on them.

## Cleaning up

It is important to keep your cat's things clean. The **bacteria** that grow on dirty things cause smells and can make cats sick. You should:

- Wash your cat's food and water bowls each week with warm, soapy water. Always wash cat dishes separately from your family's dishes.
- Clean out dirty clumps of **cat litter** from the **litter tray** each day using a special scoop.
- Completely empty the litter tray into the dustbin at least once every week. Wash the tray and scoop using a pet **disinfectant** and water. Ask at your pet shop which disinfectant is best. When the tray is clean, dry it and add fresh litter. Always wash your hands carefully when you have finished cleaning.

You will need to check the litter tray regularly to see if it needs to be cleaned out.

## Warning

You should always wear rubber gloves whenever you clean out a dirty cat litter tray. Some tiny bugs in cat **faeces** can cause serious diseases.

## Grooming your cat

Cats normally spend a lot of time cleaning their hair and skin. This is called **grooming.** Grooming removes dust, dirt, and loose hairs. Short-haired cats can groom themselves well, but long-haired cats need help. Long hair can get stuck or matted together with dirt. Long-haired cats swallow a lot of hair as they groom, forming clumps of hair called hairballs. Although most cats cough up hairballs, hairballs can sometimes block up their stomachs.

Start grooming by gently combing the hair to remove any tangles. Then use a soft brush to smooth the combed fur. Be careful around the cat's face.

## Grooming

- Most cats love to be groomed. Enjoy this time with your pet.
- You will need a metal comb and a soft bristle brush. Ask at your pet shop or vet which combs and brushes are best for your cat.
- Wear some old clothes and brush your cat over an old cloth to catch the loose hair.
- Your cat needs to be calm before you groom its belly, legs, and toes. If it is not calm, it might scratch you. Talk to your cat so that it relaxes.

## Holidays

Your cat needs to be looked after every day, even when you go on holiday. Some people take their cat with them, but this is not always possible. Most cats like to live in the place they know well. It is best to get someone you know and trust to look after your cat in your home. Alternatively, you may be able to find a professional **cat sitter** who will be able to do this job for you.

If this is impossible, you can take your cat to stay in a local **cattery**. Catteries have staff whose job it is to care for cats. You could ask a vet to recommend a place, or visit a cattery first to see what it is like. You will have to pay for the cat to stay there. You will also need to have records proving your cat has been **vaccinated** regularly (see page 37). You will also need a pet carrier to transport the cat to the cattery.

Cats are happy to stay at home when you are away, as long as someone can pop in every day to look after them.

Catteries like this provide a safe temporary home for your cat when you are not around.

## Flea protection

You may notice fleas or flea droppings when you brush your cat. Fleas are a common problem for cats. They live on cats and feed on their blood. Their tiny bites make your cat's skin itchy. You can buy powders, sprays, drops, and even flea collars at pet shops or vets to get rid of fleas. Many people use drops that you apply to the cat's back.

To get rid of fleas completely you will need to treat your house, too. Fleas lay eggs on cats but also on carpets and other surfaces. Baby fleas hatch out and can survive for months without feeding before they have the chance to jump onto a passing cat. You should vacuum carpets and curtains and wash cat bedding regularly. You can also use sprays from pet shops to treat these places.

Usually the first sign of fleas is when your cat scratches itself a lot.

## Where do fleas come from?

Cats can catch fleas from many places, including:

- other cats and dogs
- carpets, curtains, and bedding in your house if they have fleas living in them
- grass and other plants outside.

## Worms

Cats commonly have roundworms and tapeworms living inside them. Cats get worms accidentally by swallowing worm eggs off the ground or when they **groom**. The eggs hatch into adult worms in the cat's **intestines.** Worms do not seriously harm cats but may give them **diarrhoea**, make them weak or make their bottom itchy. Some warning signs that a cat has worms are a swollen belly or when a cat licks its bottom a lot.

You can treat your cat for worms by giving them worming tablets bought from a vet or a pet shop. You will need to repeat this every few months or your cat will get worms again.

It is difficult to get a cat to take a worming tablet. You should ask an adult or vet to do it.

**Did you know?**
Cat fleas can carry tapeworms, so if you get rid of fleas you also help to get rid of worms!

31

# Living with your cat

It takes a little while to get used to living with your pet cat. You need to know how to handle it properly and understand its moods. You also need to know what to do if there are any problems.

## Picking up your cat

You need to pick a cat up carefully so you don't scare or hurt it. Follow these steps:

- Put one hand under your cat's chest, just behind her front legs.
- Place the other hand under the back of her back legs.
- Lift the cat up into your bent arm to support her.
- Don't hold onto the cat if she struggles to get away when you pick her up. If you hold on, you'll make her unhappy and she may scratch or bite you.
- Do not drop the cat after holding her. Place her gently down on the floor.

## Warning

Never pick up a cat by the scruff (back) of its neck. Picking up a cat like this can damage its neck muscles.

You must support a cat properly when you pick it up.

## Petting and stroking your cat

It is important to stroke and handle your cat gently. Only do it when your cat is awake. If you touch your cat while she is sleeping, you may frighten her.

Always stroke cats in the direction that their hair grows. Most cats enjoy being stroked in particular places on their body. You could try softly under the chin, around the ears and chest, and around the neck and upper back.

A happy cat purrs loudly and closes its eyes because it is feeling very safe and comfortable.

## Togetherness

Cats usually decide when they want to be stroked and cuddled. Many cats enjoy sitting on your lap in the evening. Some may stomp on you before they settle down. Stomping is when cats use their paws to press on your clothes while purring, sometimes with their nose very close to you.

## When cats get rough

Some cats can rapidly change mood when they are being stroked. They can change from being calm to being very angry. The cat is telling you to stop! Leave it alone for now. Next time try stroking its head and neck rather than back or belly.

## Knowing your cat's moods

Cats cannot tell you how they feel using words. They show their moods by changing their face and body positions. For example, when a cat is angry or ready to attack, it lowers its head and twists its ears back. Its eyes narrow and it looks straight ahead. However, when a cat is frightened or feels unsafe, it crouches down. It lowers its ears, opens its eyes wide, and often looks away from you.

It takes time for you to understand these different signals. However, be patient and try to learn what your cat wants to tell you.

One way to tell if a cat is angry or playful is if its tail is twitching.

## Cat sounds

Cats make about eight different meow sounds. They use them to tell you different things, such as when they want food, when they want you to open a door, or even to tell you when they are unhappy. They also make spitting, hissing, and growling sounds, usually when they are frightened or angry.

Even though he can't talk, it is clear that this cat wants to go through the door.

## Keeping cats inside

Even cats that usually go outside should sometimes be kept inside to be safe.

- Try to keep cats in at night. Most traffic accidents involving cats happen at night, as do attacks on cats by wild animals.
- Never let cats out when people are letting off fireworks. Noisy fireworks frighten cats, especially nervous ones.
- If your cat is ill or wounded keep him indoors. If he goes outside it may make the problem worse.
- Don't let your cat outside if there are dangerous things around, like poisonous garden chemicals or broken glass.
- Keep your cat indoors if he has been fighting with other cats. If you keep him in for a few days, the fighting may stop.

## What to do if your cat goes missing

Cats may go missing for days or even weeks. Here are some places to check:

- Inside cupboards, cellars and attics, or under beds.
- Outside in sheds, up trees, or in neighbours' homes and gardens. (Make sure you ask an adult or your neighbour before checking these areas.)
- Your local animal **rescue centre.**
- Where your cat used to live. Some cats return long distances to previous homes.

If there is no sign of your cat, put up pictures and a description in local shops, vet's offices, and libraries. Ask friends to help you look for him.

It is safer not to let your cat out at night if possible.

35

# Cat health

Cats usually remain healthy if they are fed and cared for properly. An important part of cat care is keeping an eye on your pet's health. You will know your cat very well and soon spot any changes to his health. If you are unsure about your cat's health, ask an adult to take him to the vet to be examined. Remember that your pet can get sick quickly, so contact a vet as soon as possible.

A healthy cat will have bright, clean eyes, a pink mouth, and white teeth.

## Vet checks

It is important to take your cat to the vet each year for a check up. Vets will check the cat's ears, mouth, hair, and claws for any problems. They will also give annual **vaccinations**.

## Healthy cats

A healthy cat should be active, alert, and happy. It should have smooth, well-**groomed** fur. Its eyes should be clear, clean, and bright. Its ears should be clean and pink inside. Its teeth should be white and its gums should be pink.

## Vaccinations

Cats are at risk from three diseases: feline enteritis, feline leukaemia, and cat flu. They usually catch these diseases from other cats. The first two diseases may kill cats unless they are treated quickly. Cat flu is not always fatal, but it can make your cat sneeze and have sticky eyes.

Vaccinations stop cats getting sick in the first place. A vet injects a special fluid called a vaccine under a cat's skin. The **injection** does not hurt your cat. Vets give the first vaccination to a kitten when it is about nine weeks old. After that the cat will need a booster vaccination each year to keep it safe. You will get a certificate from the vet that proves your cat is vaccinated.

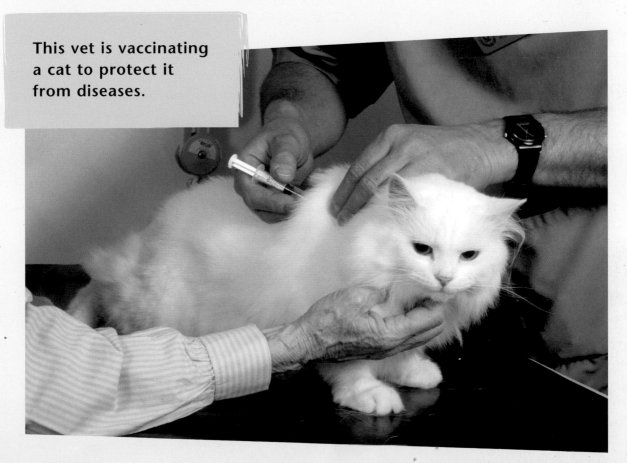

This vet is vaccinating a cat to protect it from diseases.

## Sore mouth

Wild cats naturally wipe their teeth clean as they chew **prey**. Pet cats, especially those that eat mostly soft food, cannot clean their teeth so well. **Bacteria** grow on dirty teeth leaving a yellow coating called plaque, which causes gum disease.

Cats with gum disease have bad breath and have bright red or greyish gums. They find it painful to eat. You can prevent gum disease in your cat by cleaning her teeth with cat toothpaste from a vet or pet shop. Ask an adult to rub the toothpaste on the teeth carefully using a piece of soft cloth or a pet toothbrush.

Some cats do not like having their teeth cleaned. They may bite or scratch until they get used to it. If plaque cannot be brushed off, take your cat to a vet. They will give your cat an **injection** to keep her still. She will not feel anything while the vet scrapes off the plaque.

### Top tip

Some adult cats do not like to have their teeth cleaned. Start cleaning your cat's teeth while she is young so she gets used to it. Begin with a few teeth at a time and build up until you can clean the whole mouth.

You can brush your cat's teeth to keep her mouth healthy.

## Waxy ears

Cats usually have some wax in their ears. If there is lots of dark brown, grainy wax, this may mean your cat has ear mites. Ear mites are animals that look like very tiny crabs. Ear mites irritate your cat and make her shake her head or scratch her ears roughly. Scratching can damage the skin of the ear. You can get rid of ear mites using eardrops from a vet.

The vet is making sure this cat's ears are healthy, using a special tool to look inside them.

### Warning

Never clean the inside of your cat's ears, because you might damage her hearing.

## Sore eyes

Sometimes a cat's eyes may become red and sticky with thick tears. This is a sign of an eye **infection** caused by scratching or by something rubbing under the cat's eyelid. A vet can give the cat special eye drops to clear up the infection. The vet might say that you should clean the eyes carefully using cotton wool dipped in cooled, boiled water. Ask an adult to help you.

## Third eyelid

Cats have a third eyelid called a haw. It protects the eye from drying out. If you can see the haw all the time, then your cat is ill and should be taken to the vet.

The third eyelid stops a cat's eye from getting too dry.

## Wounds

If your cat has a small wound like a bite or scratch it should heal very quickly. It will take much longer to heal if the wound gets infected. To keep a wound clean, bathe it with salty water. Use one teaspoon of salt in 250 millilitres (half a pint) of water.

If your cat has a large cut or wound, you should take him to a vet. You should also take your cat to a vet if the wound is dirty or does not start to heal within a few days. The vet will give you **antibiotic** cream to put on the cat's wound. The vet may shave the cat's hair around the wound. This stops dirt from the hair from infecting the wound.

## Stomach problems

Cats have sensitive stomachs. If they eat unusual or infected food, they may suffer from stomach problems. These include **diarrhoea**, which is runny **faeces,** and **vomiting**. Treat these problems by removing any food and by giving only small amounts of water for 24 hours. If the stomach problems last longer than this, take your cat to a vet.

A vet has put a collar on this cat to stop him licking a wound on his back. This will let the wound heal properly.

## Abscesses

An abscess is an **infection** deep under the skin. This causes a swollen lump, filled with pus, that is painful and makes your cat feel poorly. You will need to take your cat to the vet. The vet will drain the abscess and give the cat antibiotics to clear up the infection.

## Claws

If cats scratch enough, they usually keep their claws short. However, sometimes claws can get very long or break. They may hurt or catch in things more easily. Take the cat to a vet who will know how to cut claws properly.

Your cat may meow, hiss, or even try to scratch you if you touch his skin when there is a painful abscess underneath.

## Warning

Never try to cut a cat's claws yourself because you may hurt him or damage his toes.

# Growing old

Most cats live for around twelve to fifteen years, but some cats live for up to twenty years. As they grow old, cats change. Here are some of the changes:

- Their hair may become thinner and some teeth may drop out.
- They become less active.
- They may have a few more accidents around the house, leaving **urine** or **faeces** away from the **litter tray.**
- They may become grumpier.
- Some older cats may want to be stroked less, but some want more attention than ever before.

## Older health

It is important to help an older cat stay healthy. You will need to give it food designed for older cats. This food will give it energy even when the cat does not eat as much as it used to. You will probably need to take the cat to the vet more regularly than before for health check ups. Keep the cat happy by helping out with **grooming,** keeping it company, and by being patient.

Old cats may spend most of their time asleep in a favourite spot.

## The right time

Eventually, life may become miserable for a very old cat. It may not be able to recover from illness, clean itself, or eat properly. This might be the time to take the cat to the vet to end its life. The vet will give the cat gas or an **injection** that stops it breathing. Neither the gas nor the injection hurt your cat. It is kinder to end a suffering cat's life like this than to let it live on in pain or misery.

## Losing a friend

It is really hard when a pet dies. You will feel very sad because you have lost a friend. Your home may feel empty. But talk about your feelings to your family and friends. Most people will understand how you are feeling. In a few days or weeks, you will remember the good times you had with your pet.

Photographs are a good way of always remembering a much-loved pet that has died.

# Keeping a record

Pet cats usually live long and full lives. If you have a good memory, you might be able to remember a lot about your pet. But to make sure you do not forget too much, why not keep a record? Then you can remind yourself about all the happy times you shared with your cat.

## Cat scrapbook

You could buy a scrapbook or make one out of strong paper. Collect photos of your cat at different ages and paste them in. How has your cat changed over time? You could include information about your cat, such as when and where you got him from, his favourite foods, the different meows he makes, the games he likes to play, and so on.

## Diary entries

You could keep a diary section in your scrapbook where you write down what happens at different times during the cat's life, such as:

- What does your cat do when he first arrives at your home?
- When does your cat have his **vaccinations**?
- When does he go to a **cattery**?
- How many hours a day does he sleep or play?

Your scrapbook can be a record of your cat when he was just a tiny kitten!

## Find out more

You could find out a lot more information about cats, cat care, cats in history, record-breaking cats, and so on and paste it into your scrapbook. Places to look for information include the Internet and the library. You could also visit cat shows, zoos, wildlife parks, and museums to learn more about different cat **breeds** and other members of the cat family.

## Paw prints

We use human fingerprints to identify people so how about using paw prints in your cat scrapbook? Ask an adult to help you with this activity.

- Cover a table with newspaper or old cloth. Put the open scrapbook on top.
- Make up a bowl of non-toxic, water-based paint.
- Gently dip your cat's paws in the paint.
- Encourage the cat to walk across the scrapbook to leave paw prints.
- Make sure the cat does not lick its paws until you have carefully washed off the paint.
- Allow the paint to dry before closing the book.

Remember to take lots of photos of your cat, so that you can add them to your scrapbook.

# Glossary

**animal shelter**   place where abandoned or badly treated pets are cared for

**antibiotic**   medicine that can cure some animal diseases

**archaeologist**   someone who studies history by digging up ancient remains

**asthma**   condition that causes people to have breathing problems

**bacteria**   tiny living things. Some bacteria are useful, such as those found in yoghurt. Other bacteria can cause disease.

**breeder**   someone who raises a particular kind of animal

**breeds**   different kinds of cats

**calcium**   substance used by the body to build strong teeth and bones

**carnivore**   animal that eats other animals or meat from other animals

**cat litter**   material to put in litter trays to soak up urine

**cat sitter**   someone who visits people's homes to look after their cats while they are away

**catnip**   plant containing an oil that cats are strongly attracted to

**cattery**   place that looks after cats for people while they are on holiday

**deterrent**   something that stops a person or animal from doing something

**diarrhoea**   runny faeces (droppings or poo)

**disinfectant**   spray or liquid that destroys germs

**faeces**   droppings or poo

**groom**   to clean an animal's fur. Many animals groom themselves.

**house-trained**   an animal that is trained to go to the toilet outside or in a litter tray, not in the house

**infection**   illness that makes part of the body fill with pus

**injection**   when a needle is used to put medicine into an animal's body

**intestines**   part of the body that leads from the stomach to the anus

**litter**   a number of baby animals born together

**litter tray**   tray where cats can go to the toilet

**microchip**   tiny piece of material used to store a lot of information

**minerals**   different substances used by the body for various purposes

**neutered**   when part of an animal's sexual organs are removed so that it cannot reproduce (have babies)

**nutrients**   parts of food that an animal's body needs to grow and keep healthy

**pedigree**   when a purebred animal has a list of its ancestors

**prey**   animal that gets eaten by other animals

**queen**   female cat

**rescue centres**   places where abandoned pets are cared for

**rodent**   animal with strong front teeth that keep growing throughout its life

**species**   kind or type of animal

**suckle**   when a baby mammal drinks milk from its mother's body

**territory**   patch of land that an animal thinks of as its own

**tom**   male cat

**urine**   liquid waste from the body, also called wee

**vaccination**   injection that protects an animal against a disease

**vitamins**   nutrients found in food. Animals need certain vitamins to keep them healthy.

**vomit**   to be sick

**warm-blooded**   describes an animal that can warm up or cool down to adapt to its surroundings

46

# Further reading

*Care for Your Kitten (RSPCA Pet Guides)*, by Heather Thomas (editor) (Collins, 2004)

*Kitten Care (How to Look After Your Pet)* (Dorling Kindersley, 2004)

*The New Guide to Cat Care (Practical Handbook)*, by Alan Edwards (Lorenz Books, 2002)

# Useful addresses

Most countries have organizations and societies that work to protect animals from cruelty and to help people learn how to care for the pets they live with properly.

**UK**
Royal Society for the Prevention
   of Cruelty to Animals (RSPCA)
Wilberforce Way
Southwater
Horsham
West Sussex
RH13 9RS
Tel: 0870 33 35 999
Fax: 0870 75 30 284

**Australia**
RSPCA Australia Inc.
PO Box 265
Deakin West ACT 2600
Tel.: 02 6282 8300
Fax: 02 6282 8311

## Internet

There are hundreds of pet websites on the Internet. They give information about different breeds and about caring for your pet.

http://www.bbc.co.uk/cbbc/wild/pets/cat.shtml – this website from the BBC has advice sheets about cat care that can be printed out.

http://www.rspca.org.uk – the website of the UK RSPCA has lots of information about cat care. Search under "Animal care".

You can also use the Internet to find out about cat clubs in your local area.

**Disclaimer**
All the Internet addresses (URLs) given in this book were valid at the time of going to press. However, due to the dynamic nature of the Internet, some addresses may have changed, or sites may have changed or ceased to exist since publication. While the author and Publishers regret any inconvenience this may cause readers, no responsibility for any such changes can be accepted by either the author or the Publishers.

# Index

# Titles in the *Keeping Pets* series include:

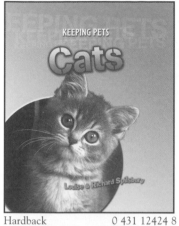

Hardback      0 431 12424 8

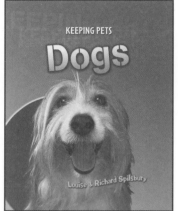

Hardback      0 431 12425 6

Hardback      0 431 12426 4

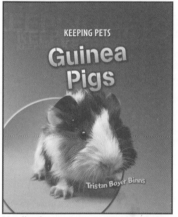

Hardback      0 431 12427 2

Hardback      0 431 12428 0

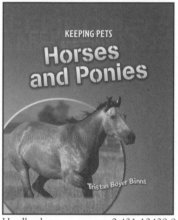

Hardback      0 431 12429 9

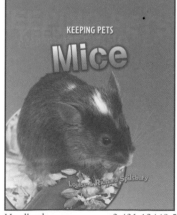

Hardback      0 431 12448 5

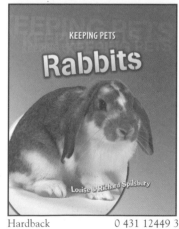

Hardback      0 431 12449 3

Find out about other titles from Heinemann Library on our website www.heinemann.co.uk/library